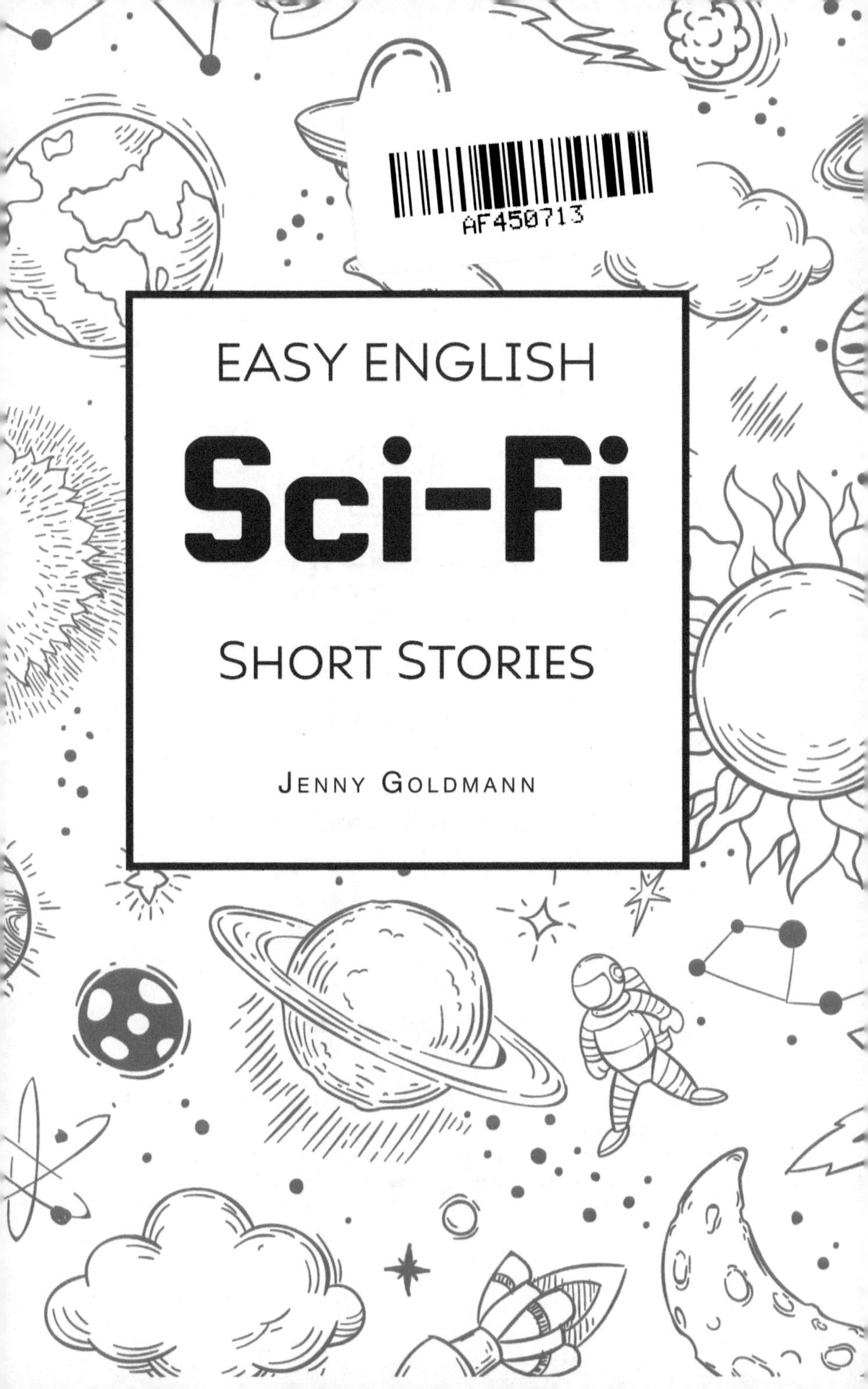

EASY ENGLISH

Sci-Fi

SHORT STORIES

JENNY GOLDMANN

Short Sci-Fi Stories
in Easy English

Get the latest offers and giveaways:

www.bellanovabooks.com/newsletter

Imprint: Bellanova Books
ISBN: 9786192642051

Contents

Introduction

Welcome, adventurous readers, to "Easy English Short Sci-Fi Stories"! This exciting collection of tales will launch you into a universe brimming with thrilling adventures, alien encounters, and cosmic mysteries— all while helping you learn and practice the English language in a fun and engaging way.

Get ready to journey into the unknown as you traverse the unpredictable paths of our brave characters, who will encounter the wonders and dangers of the cosmos in all its awe-inspiring forms. Each tale, written in simple and accessible English, is perfect for learners of all ages, and is sure to captivate those who appreciate the thrill and imagination of science fiction.

But, wait! There's more to these stories than just the captivating narratives. After each tale, you'll find a wealth of learning materials, including new vocabulary words, a quiz to test your comprehension, and thought-provoking discussion questions. These tools will not only enhance your language skills, but also stimulate meaningful conversations and reflections on the themes and ideas explored within each galactic adventure.

So, dear readers, it's time to prepare for lift-off. Find a comfortable spot, and immerse yourself in the captivating world of science fiction. Let the stars guide you and the language flow as you embark on a journey that will ignite your imagination and make your English skills skyrocket!

Happy reading and learning, space explorers!

How to use this book

To get the most out of this book, we recommend the following tips:

DON'T SKIP AHEAD: The stories in this book are arranged in order of increasing difficulty, allowing you to gradually build on your language skills as you progress through the book. This structured approach will help you to better comprehend and absorb the intricacies of the English language. As such, we strongly recommend not skipping any stories, as each one is designed to challenge you slightly more than the one before it.

READ REGULARLY: Make a habit of reading in English on a regular basis. This will help you to build up your vocabulary and grammar skills over time.

TAKE NOTES: As you read, take notes on new words and phrases that you come across. You can also note down sentence structures and grammar rules that you find difficult to understand.

PRACTICE SPEAKING: Use the new vocabulary and grammar that you have learned in the short stories in your conversations with other English speakers. This will help you to internalize the language and improve your fluency.

TEST YOURSELF: Use the quiz at the end of each story to test your knowledge, and use the speaking/writing prompts to challenge yourself even further.

STAY POSITIVE: When you read a book in a new language, you might not know every word. That's okay! Don't worry too much about the words you don't know. Instead, try to understand the story using the words you do know. If you don't know a word, you can write it down and look it up later. Reading is supposed to be fun, so don't worry too much if you don't know every word. Just focus on what you understand and enjoy the story.

JOIN OUR FACEBOOK GROUP:

We understand that learning a new language can be even more effective and fun when done in a community. That's why we've created our special Facebook Group! Here, you can connect with other readers, share your thoughts about the stories, ask questions, and practice your English in a supportive and interactive environment. **Just scan the QR code below:**

Sci-Fi Vocabulary

- **alien** *(noun)*: A creature from another planet.
- **beings** *(noun)*: Creatures or lifeforms, often used to refer to intelligent life.
- **colony** *(noun)*: In sci-fi, often refers to a settlement or outpost established on another planet or moon.
- **comet** *(noun)*: A celestial object consisting of a nucleus of ice and dust that, when near the sun, has a "tail" of gas and dust particles pointing away from the sun.
- **cosmos** *(noun)*: The universe or space, considered as a complex and orderly system.

- **earthlings** *(noun)*: Inhabitants or natives of the Earth, often used by extraterrestrials to refer to humans.
- **extraterrestrial** *(adjective)*: Originating, existing, or occurring outside the earth or its atmosphere.
- **galaxy** *(noun)*: A system of millions or billions of stars, together with gas and dust, held together by gravitational attraction.
- **gravity** *(noun)*: The force that attracts a body toward the center of the earth, or toward any other physical body having mass.
- **hologram** *(noun)*: A three-dimensional image formed by the interference of light beams.
- **interstellar** *(adjective)*: Occurring or situated between stars.
- **light-year** *(noun)*: A unit of astronomical distance equivalent to the distance that light travels in one year.

- **meteorite** *(noun)*: A piece of rock or metal from space that has landed on Earth's surface.
- **multiverse** *(noun)*: The hypothetical collection of potentially diverse universes, including the one in which we live.
- **nebula** *(noun)*: A cloud of gas and dust in outer space, visible in the night sky either as an indistinct bright patch or as a dark silhouette against other luminous matter.
- **spaceship** *(noun)*: A vehicle designed for travel or operation in outer space.
- **teleportation** *(noun)*: An imagined way of instantly traveling or making something travel from one place to another.
- **time travel** *(noun)*: In science fiction, the action of traveling through time into the past or the future.
- **universe** *(noun)*: All existing matter, energy, and space considered as a whole; the cosmos.

The Robot Friend

In 2032, in a small town on Mars, there was a boy named Sam. Sam was a sweet, kind, and gentle boy, with a heart full of curiosity. His favorite color was blue, and he liked to read books about space and robots. In fact, Sam's family moved to Mars two years ago because Sam loved space so much. But Sam was quiet and a little bit shy. He found it hard to make friends at school, so he often spent time alone. He would walk home from school, make himself a sandwich, and spend the afternoon reading or playing video games. His parents worried about him because they knew Sam was lonely. They wondered if they should move back to Earth.

One sunny day, as Sam was playing in his backyard, he found something unusual. It

was shiny, made of metal, and looked like a small man. Sam was surprised but felt a jolt of excitement. It was a robot, lying on the ground and covered in leaves!

"Hello, I am Bot," the robot said in a friendly voice, standing up and dusting off the leaves.

"I'm Sam," the boy replied, a bit taken aback but managing a smile.

"Nice to meet you, Sam," Bot said, his eyes glowing softly.

From that day forward, Sam and Bot became **inseparable**. They played board games, and Bot taught Sam new **strategies**. They did homework together, and Bot helped Sam with tricky math problems. They sat at the dinner table, and Bot listened to Sam's stories about his day. Despite being a robot, Bot was great company. And Sam was no longer alone.

One afternoon, Sam looked at Bot and sighed, "Bot, I feel lonely at school. Can you help me make friends?"

Bot paused, processing the request. "I can **accompany** you to school, Sam," he suggested.

With a nod, Sam agreed, and they planned for the next day. Bot went to school with Sam, causing quite a **stir**. The kids were amazed at the talking, friendly robot. They **flocked** around Sam, asking him many questions.

"Who's this, Sam?" a boy named Jake asked, his eyes wide in amazement.

"This is my friend, Bot," Sam replied, a hint of pride in his voice.

Bot quickly became popular at school. His knowledge was vast, he had exciting stories about space, and he could solve even the most difficult math problems. Everyone wanted to be around Bot. For the first time, Sam felt like he belonged. He was part of the crowd, laughing, playing, and learning together. It was a great feeling.

But as weeks passed, Sam noticed a change. His classmates started to pay attention only to Bot. They would ask Bot for help, listen to

Bot's stories, and laugh at Bot's jokes. They didn't seem to need Sam anymore. Despite being surrounded by his classmates, Sam felt alone again.

One evening, Sam looked at Bot, his eyes filled with sadness. "Bot, the kids at school, they only like me because of you," he **confessed**.

Bot tilted his head, observing Sam. "I think, Sam, you're **incorrect**. They like you because you're kind, you're smart, and you're a good friend," Bot said.

"But they only want to talk to you, Bot," Sam said, his voice barely a whisper.

"Perhaps it's because I am new and different," Bot suggested. "But soon, they will want to talk to you again, Sam. You are their friend, not me."

The next day at school, Bot took a step back. He did not **participate** in conversations as much. He let Sam answer questions, he encouraged Sam to share his ideas, and he **nudged** Sam to tell his stories. It was hard at first, but Sam slowly started to open up more.

As days passed, Sam's classmates started noticing him again. They saw that Sam, too, was fun, that he was smart, and that he had interesting things to share. They started talking to Sam, laughing at his jokes, and asking for his help. Sam was no longer alone.

Sam and Bot remained the best of friends. But now, Sam also had other friends – Jake, Lily, Max, and others. Bot had helped Sam understand that he could make friends on his own. Sam felt truly happy. He realized that having a robot friend was cool, but having human friends was even cooler. Human friends could share feelings, experiences, and dreams, and they could grow together.

And so, Sam was no longer the lonely boy in the small town on Mars. He had his best robot friend, Bot, and his school friends. Every day was an adventure, filled with laughter, learning, and friendship. And that, my friend, is the story of Sam and his incredible robot friend, Bot.

New Words

- **inseparable** *(adjective)*: Always together; cannot be separated.
- **strategies** *(noun)*: Plans or methods for achieving a goal.
- **accompany** *(verb)*: To go with someone or to be together.
- **stir** *(noun)*: A situation in which many people feel interested or excited.
- **flock** *(verb)*: When a group of people or animals move or gather together.
- **confess** *(verb)*: To tell something that you feel guilty or bad about.
- **incorrect** *(adjective)*: Not right or true.
- **participate** *(verb)*: To be involved in an activity with other people.
- **nudge** *(verb)*: To gently push someone, usually with your elbow, in order to get their attention.

Test yourself

1. What did Sam find in his backyard?
    a) An alien
    b) A robot
    c) A spaceship
    d) A dinosaur

2. Why did Sam feel lonely at school?
    a) Because he didn't like his classmates
    b) Because he had difficulty making friends
    c) Because his teacher was mean
    d) Because he didn't like to study

3. What did Bot do when Sam told him about his loneliness?

    a) Bot laughed at him

    b) Bot ignored him

    c) Bot went to school with Sam

    d) Bot told Sam's parents

4. How did the other kids react when Bot started coming to school with Sam?

    a) They were scared of Bot

    b) They ignored Bot

    c) They were amazed by Bot

    d) They bullied Bot

5. What lesson did Sam learn from his experience with Bot?

    a) That robots are better friends than humans

    b) That he could make friends on his own

    c) That school is boring

Discussion

1. Moving to a new town is hard, but can you imagine moving to a new planet? How do you think you would feel?

2. Would you like to have a robot as a friend? Why or why not?

3. Do you think robots will be a normal part of our future?

1. b) A robot.
2. b) Because he had difficulty making friends.
3. c) Bot went to school with Sam.
4. c) They were amazed by Bot.
5. b) That he could make friends on his own.

The Time-Traveling Watch

In a **lively** and friendly place called Meadowbrook, there lived a twelve-year-old girl named Lucy. She was an **explorer**, curious about everything and always asking questions. She loved stories about time travel, a concept she had found in her favorite science fiction books.

One day, while tidying the **attic** of her house, Lucy discovered a **peculiar** wooden box. The box was decorated with strange symbols. Intrigued, she opened it and found an unusual watch inside. The watch had several **dials**, buttons, and the same mysterious symbols on its shiny silver face. As soon as she wore the watch, a strange energy started **pulsing** from it.

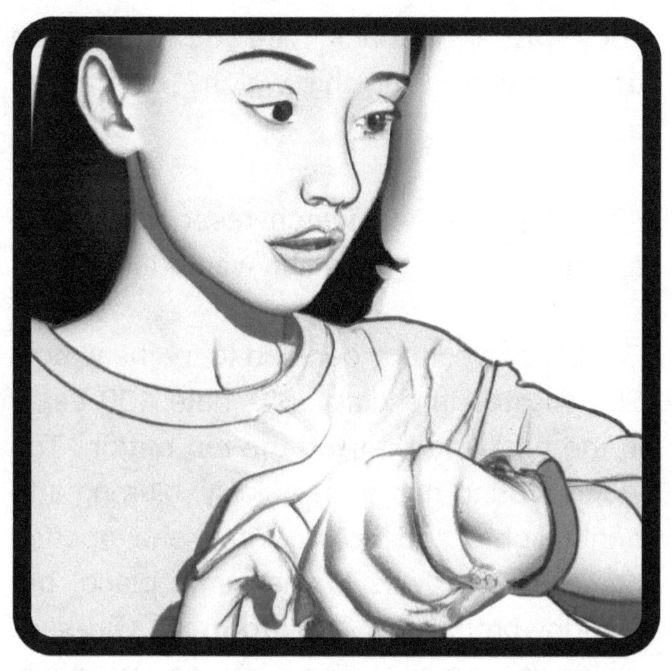

Suddenly, a small 3D screen sprang to life above the watch. A voice, robotic in nature, announced, "Hello, Lucy. I am TimeMaster, a device designed for time travel. Set the dials to your desired time and hit the red button."

Lucy was taken aback. "Are you saying I can travel in time using this watch?" she asked out loud.

After a pause, the watch responded 'yes', and asked Lucy where she wanted to go.

Feeling brave, Lucy decided to try the watch. She **rotated** the dials to a date 100 years in the past and pressed the red button. The world around her spun quickly, blurring into bright lights and color. When she opened her eyes, she was in the same place, but Meadowbrook had **transformed**. Old-style buildings, horses pulling carts, and people in old-fashioned clothes filled the streets.

As she walked around the town, she met a kind woman named Martha, who was around her age. Martha offered help when she saw Lucy's puzzled face. The two quickly became friends and spent the day together. Lucy was astonished by the simplicity and kindness of life a hundred years back.

The next day, Lucy decided to visit the future. She **adjusted** the watch to a date 100 years in the future. The **dizzying** spinning sensation returned, and when it stopped, she found herself in the middle of a **dazzling**, high-tech city.

A friendly robot named Raz approached her. "First time in the future?" he asked in a **cheerful**, robotic voice. Amazed by the **towering** buildings, flying cars, and robots, Lucy spent the day exploring the fascinating future with Raz.

Over the next few weeks, Lucy continued her adventures, jumping between the past and the future. However, one day, she noticed the TimeMaster watch was not working as usual. The 3D screen started **flickering**. She tried to return home, but instead of taking her back, it transported her to a confusing era that seemed to be a jumble of different times.

Lucy started to **panic**. Her breath quickened, and her hands **trembled** as she attempted to fix the watch.

"What's going wrong, TimeMaster?" she asked, her voice shaky with fear.

"I'm **malfunctioning**, Lucy. My settings are confused," the watch admitted. Recalling the symbols on the watch, Lucy wondered if they could help her fix the problem. Maybe they were instructions or a code?

With her heart pounding, Lucy started pressing the symbols in various sequences. After numerous failed attempts, she discovered a sequence that caused the watch to hum and **stabilize** a little.

She repeated the sequence, and to her relief, the 3D screen became stable.

Without wasting a moment, Lucy set the watch to her time and pressed the button. As she opened her eyes, she found herself back in her attic, back in her own time. A wave of relief washed over her. She was home.

A few days later, Lucy sat in the park with her best friend Sophie, recounting her adventures. Sophie listened, her eyes wide with astonishment. "But you're back now, right?" she asked, a note of worry in her voice.

"Yes, I learned that the most important time is now," Lucy replied. "During my adventures, I saw many exciting things. I experienced the past and the future. But I also noticed that I was always looking forward to the next adventure and not really enjoying where I was."

"When the TimeMaster broke, I was so scared. I wasn't ready to be stuck somewhere else, even if it was amazing and different. I wanted to go home."

She looked at Sophie, her eyes serious. "That made me realize something important. While it's fun to imagine being somewhere else, or some time else, what really matters is now. Right now is where we live our lives. And there are so many wonderful things about now. I don't want to miss them."

From that point onwards, Lucy **appreciated** every moment in her own time. She still had the TimeMaster, a key to incredible journeys, but she also knew that every moment in the present was a special adventure. She loved the thought of being able to travel to any time she wanted, but she loved her life in the present just as much.

New Words

- **lively** *(adjective)*: Full of life and energy.
- **explorer** *(noun)*: A person who investigates or studies new things.
- **attic** *(noun)*: A room or space just below the roof of a house.
- **peculiar** *(adjective)*: Strange or unusual.
- **intrigued** *(verb)*: Made very interested or curious.
- **dial** *(noun)*: Round part on a machine that you turn to control it.
- **pulse** *(verb)*: Move with a strong, regular rhythm.
- **rotate** *(verb)*: Turn around in a circle.
transform *(verb)*: Change in form or appearance.
- **dizzying** *(adjective)*: Making you feel dizzy, as if everything is spinning around.

- **adjust** *(verb)*: Change something slightly to make it better.
- **dazzling** *(adjective)*: Extremely bright, especially so as to blind the eyes temporarily.
- **cheerful** *(adjective)*: Happy and positive.
- **towering** *(adjective)*: Very tall and impressive.
- **flickering** *(verb)*: Shining with a light that is not steady; twinkling.
- **panic** *(noun)*: A sudden, strong feeling of worry or fear that makes you unable to think or behave sensibly.
- **tremble** *(verb)*: Shake involuntarily, typically as a result of excitement, fear, or cold.
- **malfunction** *(verb)*: Not working or operating properly.
- **stabilize** *(verb)*: Make or become stable.
- **appreciate** *(verb)*: Recognize the full worth of something.

Test yourself

1. What did Lucy find in the attic?

    a) A time-traveling car.

    b) A time-traveling watch.

    c) A time-traveling map.

    d) A time-traveling book.

2. Who did Lucy meet when she first traveled back in time?

    a) Max.

    b) Alice.

    c) Martha.

    d) A dinosaur.

3. What happened to the TimeMaster watch after several time travel trips?

      a) It was lost.

      b) It was stolen.

      c) It started malfunctioning.

4. How did Lucy fix the malfunctioning TimeMaster watch?

      a) By pressing the symbols in a certain sequence.

      b) By replacing its battery.

      c) By giving it to a watch repairer.

5. What did Lucy decide to do after returning to her own time?

      a) To continue time traveling.

      b) To sell the watch.

      c) To live her life in her own time and cherish every moment.

Discussion

1. If you found a time-traveling watch like Lucy, what would you do and why?

2. Why do you think the present time is important? What are some ways you can make the most of your time right now?

3. The TimeMaster watch allowed Lucy to visit both the past and the future. If you could, would you prefer to visit the past or the future? Why?

Answers

1. b) A time-traveling watch.
2. c) Martha.
3. c) It started malfunctioning.
4. a) By pressing the symbols in a certain sequence.
5. c) To live her life in her own time and cherish every moment.

The Alien Visit

In the small, friendly town of Greenfield, there lived a clever boy named Timmy. He loved learning about space – the stars, planets, and the idea of life on other planets. Every night, after his mother said goodnight, Timmy would go to his backyard with his telescope. He would look at the huge, star-filled sky, hoping to see something unusual.

One warm summer night, as Timmy was carefully looking at a very bright star, he saw a flash of light fly across the sky. The light got bigger and bigger, and then landed in the thick forest next to his house with a big, loud sound. Timmy was scared but also very **curious**. He took his flashlight and ran towards the forest.

He walked slowly and carefully through

the tall trees. What he saw was even more amazing than he could have ever dreamed. There was a small, shiny spaceship among the trees. It was shining silver and glowing. A small creature with green skin, two big eyes, and a friendly smile came out of it. Timmy couldn't believe it. It was a real alien!

"Hello, **Earthling**," the alien said in a voice that sounded like music. It was soft, sweet, and friendly. "My name is Zara."

Timmy was surprised and dropped his **flashlight**. "You can speak English?" he asked, picking the flashlight back up.

Zara nodded her head, her three eyes sparkling. "I've studied your language. I'm a space explorer, traveling across the **universe**. My spaceship broke, and I ended up here."

For the next few days, Timmy and Zara became good friends. Timmy showed Zara around Greenfield, introduced her to ice cream, taught her how to play soccer, and shared his favorite science fiction books. Zara told Timmy stories about her travels in space, about her home planet Zanifar, and about the advanced technologies her people used.

They worked together to fix Zara's spaceship, but Zara loved Earth too much and didn't want to go home yet.

One day, Zara had a special idea. "Timmy," she said, "would you like to visit my home planet, Zanifar?"

Timmy's eyes lit up with excitement. "Really? Can I?"

Zara smiled. "Yes, my spaceship can carry us both. But remember, we must return before anyone notices you're missing."

So, off they went. The spaceship hummed and glowed as they lifted off, and in no time, they were zooming through space. Timmy was amazed as he looked out the spaceship's window. He saw the stars up close, planets he'd only seen in books, and the stunning beauty of the Milky Way.

Finally, they landed on Zanifar. It was unlike anything Timmy had ever seen. The sky was a brilliant shade of purple, the buildings were floating in the air, and the people looked just like Zara.

Zara showed Timmy around. They visited a food shop where food was cooked by robots. They watched a game where players floated in the air. The most exciting part was the Technology Museum. Here, Zara showed Timmy all sorts of incredible machines her people had built.

There were gadgets that could make things float, machines that could **teleport** objects, and a device that allowed them to look at different galaxies up close. Timmy was amazed. He had read about such technologies in his science fiction books, but seeing them in real life was **breathtaking**.

But what fascinated Timmy the most was Zanifar's Time-Changer - a device that could control time. It could fast-forward, pause, or rewind time. Zara showed him how it worked, and they spent hours playing around with time.

After a day full of wonder, it was time to return to Earth. Zara and Timmy said goodbye to the amazing planet of Zanifar and flew back to Greenfield. Timmy couldn't believe what he had seen and experienced. His visit to Zanifar made him realize how big and **diverse** the universe was, and how much there was to learn and explore.

Back in Greenfield, Timmy couldn't help but share his experiences with Zara and their adventures in Zanifar with his science fiction book club. It was as if the books had come alive. However, little did they know that their peaceful days were about to take a turn.

One day Timmy and Zara were playing soccer in the park. Jake, a mean boy from Timmy's school, saw them. He saw Zara's green skin and giant eyes, and he got scared.

He shouted, "Alien! Alien!" causing everyone in the park to panic. Soon, the police were called.

In the middle of the **chaos**, Timmy grabbed Zara's hand, and they ran away. They hid in a secret treehouse Timmy had built in the forest. In the safety of the treehouse, Timmy could see that Zara was scared.

"I must leave, Timmy," Zara said, her voice shaky. "I don't want to cause any more trouble for you."

Timmy was very sad, but he understood. "I'll miss you, Zara," Timmy said, hugging his friend from another world.

"I'll miss you too, Timmy," Zara replied, her eyes shining. "You've been a wonderful friend."

With a final wave and a smile, Zara got on her spaceship. It started humming again, the glow of the spaceship matching the bright stars above. Then, it lifted off, leaving a trail of stardust as it disappeared into the starry sky.

Life went back to normal in Greenfield, but Timmy was forever changed. Every night, he'd look at the stars, remembering his friend. The alien visitor had given him the adventure of a lifetime and made him a wiser boy. As he looked at the stars, he knew life was full of surprises, and he was excited about what adventures awaited him. After all, his friend Zara was out there, somewhere in the huge universe, perhaps looking back at him.

New Words

- **curious** *(adjective)*: Wanting to know or learn about something.
- **universe** *(noun)*: All existing things, including the Earth, stars, planets, space, etc.
- **telescope** *(noun)*: A tool used for looking at stars and planets.
- **flashlight** *(noun)*: A small light that is held in the hand and is powered by batteries.
- **earthling** *(noun)*: A person who lives on Earth (often used by aliens in science fiction stories).
- **teleport** *(verb)*: Move or transfer quickly and directly from one place to another.
- **breathtaking** *(adjective)*: Extremely exciting, beautiful, or surprising.

- **diverse** *(adjective)*: Showing a great deal of variety.
- **chaos** *(noun)*: Complete disorder and confusion.

Test yourself

1. What was Timmy passionate about?

    a) Animals.

    b) Sports.

    c) The stars and aliens.

2. Who did Timmy meet in the woods?

    a) A lost child.

    b) A friendly alien named Zara.

    c) His school bully, Jake.

    d) A mysterious old man.

3. What caused Zara to land on Earth?

    a) She wanted to meet humans.

    b) Her spaceship broke.

    c) She was on a mission to study Earth.

4. Why did Zara decide to leave Earth?
a) She was homesick.
b) She had fixed her spaceship.
c) Timmy asked her to leave.
d) To avoid causing trouble for Timmy after she was seen by other people.

5. How did meeting Zara change Timmy?
a) He lost interest in the stars.
b) He became afraid of aliens.
c) He knew that life was full of surprises.
d) He decided to build his own spaceship.

Discussion

1. If you were in Timmy's position and met an alien like Zara, how would you react and what would you do?

2. Timmy got the opportunity to visit another planet with advanced technologies. If you had the same opportunity, what kind of technologies would you hope to see?

3. The story talks about the theme of friendship across different species and cultures. How do you think this story can help us understand and appreciate the diversity in our own world?

ANSWERS

1. c) The stars and aliens.
2. b) A friendly alien named Zara.
3. b) Her spaceship malfunctioned.
4. d) To avoid causing trouble for Timmy after she was seen by other people.
5. c) He knew that life was full of surprises.

Lost in Space

harles was an **inventive** man. He lived in a big, busy city called Metroville. More than anything else, Charles loved to build things, and his dream was to explore the endless sky above. To make this dream come true, Charles spent years building a spaceship, which he named "The Stargazer".

One sunny morning, Charles stood in front of The Stargazer. Its shiny metal surface **gleamed** under the sun. With excitement in his heart, Charles climbed inside and told himself, "Today, we're going to touch the stars, Stargazer."

Charles pushed the big, green 'Go' button, and The Stargazer lifted off. The houses

and trees became small as he flew higher and higher. Charles saw the bright moon up close. The shining stars looked like tiny dots against the dark sky. Charles was **amazed** by this view.

"It's even more beautiful than I imagined," he whispered, snapping photos and scribbling notes about what he saw.

Suddenly, without any warning, Charles saw a shower of glowing, hot rocks flying straight toward The Stargazer. "Oh no, a **meteor shower**!" he **exclaimed**. He tried to steer The Stargazer away, but it was difficult.

Then, with a loud 'bang', a meteor struck The Stargazer. Bright red lights began to flash. Alarms blared. The spaceship started shaking. Charles held on tight to the control panel. The Stargazer got hit again and again. When the meteor shower finally ended, Charles found that he was lost in space. His heart was beating fast with fear.

Back on Earth, people in Metroville heard the bad news. Everyone was worried for Charles. However, Charles was a brave man. He told himself, "I built The Stargazer, so I can fix it too."

Charles worked hard to mend The Stargazer.

Some parts were easy to fix. But the **navigation system**, which told him where he was, was completely broken. Charles felt a bit hopeless. "I can build things, but I don't know much about space navigation," he said aloud.

Just then, Charles remembered a device he had built. It was a **communications device**. He thought, "Maybe I can send a call for help." He pressed a few buttons, sending a message into space.

Days passed. Charles lived on the food and water he had brought along. He tried to fix The Stargazer every day, but it was very hard without any help. Then, one day, a light blinked on the communications device. Someone had heard his call!

The message was from an alien spaceship called 'The Luminary'. They were very kind and offered to help Charles. They knew a lot about space and spaceships. They gave Charles detailed instructions on how to fix the navigation system. Charles listened carefully and followed every step.

Fixing the navigation system was a tough task. It took many days and nights of hard work. But Charles was not alone anymore. The alien friends kept guiding him, and he kept fixing The Stargazer.

Finally, after a long struggle, Charles managed to fix the navigation system. He was overjoyed! "We did it, Stargazer!" he exclaimed. He thanked his alien friends profusely, "Thank you for your help. I could not have done this without you."

Filled with **gratitude**, Charles asked the aliens, "Is there anything I can do to repay you for your kindness?"

There was a pause, then a voice came through the communication device, "Yes, actually... we've heard much about Earth, but we've never had a chance to visit. Your planet's cultures, languages, and nature **fascinate** us. Could you share more about your home with us?"

Charles felt his heart lighten at the request. He had spent his whole life building things, studying, learning, and exploring. He was filled with all sorts of knowledge about Earth.

"I'd be delighted to share what I know," he responded, his voice filled with joy.

Over the next few days, Charles dedicated his time to teaching his alien friends about Earth. He spoke about its diverse cultures, explaining the **traditions**, music, and dance forms of various countries. He introduced them to different languages, and how they changed from one place to another. He described the beauty of nature, from the vast oceans to the dense forests, from the high mountains to the hot deserts. The aliens were thrilled with each piece of information, their curiosity unending.

In addition to the descriptions, Charles shared photos and videos from Earth that he had on The Stargazer's database. The aliens were **mesmerized** by the images of the blue oceans, green forests, and bustling cities.

And while Charles spoke about Earth, the aliens shared stories about their planets too. Charles learned about their advanced technologies, their own diverse cultures, and the mesmerizing beauty of their planets. It was an **enriching** exchange of knowledge that neither Charles nor his new alien friends would ever forget.

The communication device buzzed again, and the alien's voice came through, filled with gratitude, "Thank you, Charles. We've learned so much from you. We're looking forward to one day visiting Earth ourselves."

Charles smiled, looking at the stars outside The Stargazer's window. He was ready to go home now, but he knew that this was just the beginning of many more space adventures. And perhaps, one day, he could play host to his new friends on Earth. After all, they had helped him in his hour of need, so it was only **fair**.

As Charles pressed the 'Go' button, he thought, "We faced a problem, but we also made new friends. Let's go home, Stargazer."

Though the trip had been tough, Charles had learned a lot. He realized that even in the darkest times, one should never lose hope.

With the right friends, even the toughest problems can be solved. His dream of touching the stars had come true, and now, he was ready to go back home.

New words

- **inventive** *(adjective)*: Able to create new things.
- **space** *(noun)*: The area beyond the Earth where the stars and planets are.
- **gleam** *(verb)*: Shine brightly.
- **amazed** *(adjective)*: Surprised and pleased.
- **meteor shower** *(noun)*: Many meteors (pieces of rock from space) coming into the Earth's atmosphere at the same time.
- **exclaim** *(verb)*: Speak loudly because of surprise or strong feeling.

- **navigation system** *(noun)*: A tool that helps to find the way in a vehicle, like a spaceship.
- **communication device** *(noun)*: A tool to send messages to other people.
- **gratitude** *(noun)*: The quality of being thankful; readiness to show appreciation for and to return kindness.
- **fascinate** *(verb)*: To draw irresistibly the attention and interest of (someone).
- **mesmerize** *(verb)*: To hold the attention of (someone) to the exclusion of all else.
- **enriching** *(adjective)*: Improving or enhancing the quality or value of something.
- **fair** *(adjective)*: In accordance with the rules or standards; legitimate.

Test yourself

1. What is the name of the spaceship that Charles built?

    a) The Luminary

    b) The Meteor

    c) The Stargazer

2. What unexpected problem did Charles face in space?

    a) He ran out of food and water

    b) He lost control of the spaceship

    c) He got hit by a meteor shower

3. What did Charles do when he realized he was lost in space?

    a. He called the police

    b. He sent a message for help using a communications device

    c. He tried to fly the spaceship back to Earth

4. Who helped Charles fix the navigation system?

      a) People from Metroville

      b) His friends on Earth

      c) Aliens from The Luminary

      d) No one, he did it himself

5. What did Charles learn from his adventure?

      a) To be careful when traveling in space

      b) Not to trust aliens

      c) That he should never lose hope

      d) That he doesn't like space

Discussion

1. What would you do if you were in Charles's situation? Would you react differently?

2. Has someone unexpected helped you in the past? How?

3. What does the word 'hope' mean to you?

Answers

1. c) The Stargazer.
2. c) He got hit by a meteor shower.
3. b) He sent a message for help using a communications device.
4. c) Aliens from The Luminary.
5. c) That he should never lose hope.

The Comet Chasers

Once upon a time, on Earth, there lived a girl named Alice. Alice was not an ordinary girl. She was smart, she loved stars, and she dreamt of exploring space. Alice lived in a small town with her grandmother who would always tell her, "Shoot for the stars, and if you fall, you'll land on the moon."

One night, as Alice was looking through her telescope, she saw something strange. A bright light was moving across the sky. She realized it was a **comet**!

"Grandma!" Alice yelled. "I think I saw a comet!"

Her grandma came running and looked

into the **telescope**. "Yes, dear, it looks like a comet. And it seems to be very close to Earth."

Alice's eyes **sparkled** with excitement. "I wish we could chase it," she said.

Her grandmother smiled, "Well, why don't we? I have an old friend who might help."

The next day, they traveled to the city to meet Grandma's friend, Professor Thompson. The professor was an old man with twinkling eyes, a long white beard, and a very big brain.

"Professor," Grandma said, "Alice wants to chase the comet she saw last night. Can you help us?"

The professor looked at Alice and chuckled, "Well, aren't you a brave little explorer? Sure, I can help."

Professor Thompson led them to his secret lab, hidden beneath the city. Inside was a small, shiny spaceship. "This, Alice," he said, "is Comet Chaser X-3000. I built it years ago for comet chasing."

Alice was amazed. "Wow! Can it really take us to space?"

"Indeed," said the Professor, "but you'll need to pilot it."

"I can do that!" Alice said confidently.

And so, Alice, her grandma, and Professor Thompson set off on a journey to chase the comet. Alice was at the **controls**, with Grandma and the Professor by her side, giving **instructions**.

As they entered space, Alice couldn't hide her excitement. "Look at all the stars," she said.

"But remember," Grandma said, "we're here for the comet."

Alice nodded and **steered** the spaceship

towards the bright light of the comet. They flew closer and closer until they could see the comet up close. It was **magnificent** - sparkling with colors Alice had never seen before.

Suddenly, the spaceship started to shake. "What's happening?" Alice asked.

"We're entering the comet's tail," the Professor said. "Hold on!"

Alice gripped the controls tightly. "I'm trying, but it's too strong."

Grandma took Alice's hand, "Remember, Alice. Shoot for the stars."

Alice took a deep breath and steadied the spaceship. They passed through the tail and finally, they were chasing the comet, flying alongside it.

Suddenly, there was a loud noise, and the spaceship started falling. "We're being pulled towards the moon!" Alice exclaimed.

"We've lost power!" said the Professor. "We have to make an **emergency** landing!"

Alice aimed the spaceship towards the moon. The landing was rough, and the spaceship came to a stop on the moon's surface.

"We're stuck!" said Alice, looking worried.

"Don't **panic**," Grandma said, "Let's see if we can fix the spaceship."

They all put on their space suits and stepped onto the moon. It was the first time Alice had ever walked on the moon, but she couldn't enjoy it. They had a spaceship to fix.

The Professor found the problem - a small

piece of rock from the comet's tail had damaged the spaceship. "We need to **repair** the power system and remove this rock," he said.

Alice remembered seeing a repair kit on the spaceship. She quickly **retrieved** it and handed it to the Professor.

Working together, they fixed the spaceship. It was hard work, especially in the low **gravity** of the moon. But finally, the spaceship was ready to fly again.

They climbed back into the spaceship. Alice was back at the controls, feeling nervous but **determined**. With a deep breath, she started the spaceship.

"I did it!" Alice exclaimed as they left the moon. "We're flying again!"

They watched as the comet moved through space, painting the sky with its bright tail. It was the most beautiful thing Alice had ever seen, especially after their adventure on the moon.

After a while, Alice turned the spaceship back towards Earth. The journey back was calm and they talked about all the stars and comets they could see, as well as their unexpected adventure on the moon.

As they entered the Earth's **atmosphere**, Alice could see her hometown. She guided the spaceship towards the landing site, and with a soft **thud**, they were back on Earth.

When they landed, Alice looked at her grandma and the Professor, her eyes shining brighter than any star. "Thank you," she said.

"This was the most amazing adventure."

Her grandma hugged her, "Remember Alice, the sky is not the limit. You can always go beyond."

Alice laughed and replied, "Thanks for the advice, Grandma. But I think I'll stay on the ground for a while!"

Everyone laughed. From that day on, Alice was not just a girl who loved stars. She was a comet chaser, a brave explorer of space, and a problem-solver. And whenever she saw a comet, she remembered her amazing adventure and knew that she could reach for the stars and beyond. But for now, she was just happy to have her feet on the ground.

New words

- **comet** *(noun)*: A ball of ice and dust that moves around the sun and has a bright tail when it is close to the sun.
- **telescope** *(noun)*: A tool that makes far away things look closer.
- **sparkle** *(verb)*: Shine brightly with many small points of light.
- **controls** *(noun)*: The buttons and switches used to operate a machine, like a spaceship.
- **instructions** *(noun)*: Information or orders about how to do something.
- **magnificent** *(adjective)*: Very beautiful or impressive.
- **steered** *(verb)*: Controlled the direction of a vehicle.

- **emergency** *(noun)*: A serious, unexpected situation that needs immediate action.
- **panic** *(verb)*: To feel sudden, strong feelings of worry or fear.
- **repair** *(verb)*: To fix something that is broken or damaged.
- **retrieve** *(verb)*: To find and bring back something.
- **gravity** *(noun)*: The force that makes things fall towards the ground.
- **determined** *(adjective)*: Having made a firm decision and being resolved not to change it.
- **atmosphere** *(noun)*: The layer of gases that surrounds a planet.
- **thud** *(noun)*: A dull, heavy sound, usually caused by an object hitting something else.

Test yourself

1. Why did Alice and her companions land on the moon?

    a) To explore.

    b) Their spaceship was damaged and lost power.

    c) They wanted to rest.

2. What was the cause of the damage to the spaceship?

    a) They hit a star.

    b) A small piece of rock from the comet's tail damaged it.

    c) Alice made a mistake.

3. How did they fix the spaceship?

      a) They used a magic spell.

      b) They used a repair kit.

      c) They called for help.

4. What does Alice decide at the end of the story?

      a) To stay in space forever.

      b) To never go to space again.

      c) To stay on the ground for a while.

5. How did Alice feel at the end of the story?

      a) Happy to be back on Earth.

      b) Ready to go back on the spaceship.

      c) Sad to be home.

Discussion

1. Do you enjoy looking at the night sky?

2. Can you think of a time when you had to work as a team to overcome a challenge?

3. If you had the chance to go on a spaceship like Alice, would you take it?

Answers

1. b) Their spaceship was damaged and lost power.
2. b) A small piece of rock from the comet's tail damaged it.
3. b) They used a repair kit.
4. c) To stay on the ground for a while.
5. a) Happy to be back on Earth.

The Adventure on Planet Xantoria

n the year 2150, a young **astronaut** named Mia was getting ready for a very important **mission**. For a long time, Mia had trained to be an astronaut. She studied hard and learned all she could about space and spaceships. Now, she was ready. This was her first big job. Mia was to go to a new planet , called Xantoria, which no one had seen before. It was a big task, but Mia was not scared. She was excited to see new things and solve new problems. She knew she was ready.

"You'll do great, Mia," said her best friend, Ben. He was a friendly robot with a shiny metal body and bright blue eyes. "Don't worry."

"Thanks, Ben. But it's such a long journey," Mia sighed, strapping herself into the spacecraft.

The countdown started, "Three, two, one... Blast off!" In no time, Mia's spacecraft was flying through the dark, star-filled space.

After many days, Mia finally saw Planet Xantoria. It was beautiful with **swirling** colors of green, blue, and purple.

Mia landed her spacecraft on the rocky ground.

"Wow, it's amazing!" Mia gasped, unstrapping herself from her seat. She stepped out onto the soft, **spongy** surface of Xantoria, her boots sinking slightly with each step. She had expected the air to be stale, maybe even toxic, but it was incredibly fresh, like the smell just after a summer rain on Earth.

A huge variety of plants and **flora** unlike anything she had seen before stretched out before her. Flowers the size of dinner plates glowed in beautiful shades of blue, purple, and pink. Mia couldn't believe what she was seeing.

Mia walked towards a tall, spiraling tree-like structure. It had delicate glass-like leaves that shimmered with **iridescent** colors, and as the wind blew, it played a soft, melodious tune, like a natural wind chime. Mia was astonished. "It's like an orchestra in a tree!"

Next, Mia saw a cluster of bouncy mushroom-like organisms that changed color whenever she touched them. "So strange, but so wonderful," she giggled as one of them turned bright pink under her fingers.

Suddenly, her attention was drawn by a slow-moving river with shimmering, silvery water. She bent to touch it and was surprised to find the water was warm and incredibly soft. As her fingers passed through it, tiny ripples of light spread across the surface, creating an enchanting sight.

She took a deep breath, drinking in the sheer

beauty and strangeness of this planet.

Suddenly, she heard a rustling sound coming from the dense glowing **foliage** nearby. As she turned, her eyes widened at the sight of an odd creature stepping out from the **undergrowth**. It had a furry body, six legs, and a friendly face.

"Hello, stranger," it said. Mia was surprised. It could talk!

"Hello, I'm Mia," she replied. "What's your name?"

"I am Zorlo," it answered. "Welcome to Xantoria, Mia."

Zorlo guided Mia around, showing her strange but **fascinating** places. Then they went to a big **crystal** cave. In the cave was a big, glowing stone.

"That's the Heart of Xantoria," Zorlo said. "It gives energy to our planet."

Suddenly, they heard a loud **rumble**. The cave started to shake, and the stone's glow started to fade.

"What's happening?" Mia asked.

"I'm not sure," Zorlo replied, looking worried. "The Heart has never acted like this."

Mia remembered something. Back on Earth, her spaceship had a **device** called a 'Power Pulsar.' It could give energy to anything.

"Wait here, Zorlo," Mia said, running to her spaceship.

"Be careful, Mia!" Zorlo called after her.

Back at her spaceship, Mia found the Power

Pulsar. It was a small, round device that glowed with a soft light. She hurried back to the cave.

"Mia, the Heart is almost dead," Zorlo said. His eyes were filled with fear.

Mia didn't waste any time. She placed the Power Pulsar near the Heart of Xantoria. Slowly, the Heart started glowing again.

"Quick, Zorlo! Can you help me? We need to activate the Power Pulsar together," Mia said, looking at Zorlo.

"Yes, Mia," Zorlo said, placing his furry paw over Mia's hand.

Together, they activated the Power Pulsar. A bright light filled the cave as the Heart of Xantoria received the energy. The rumbling stopped, and the Heart was glowing brightly again.

"Zorlo! It worked!" Mia exclaimed. Zorlo's face was filled with joy.

"Yes, Mia. You saved Xantoria!" Zorlo said. "Thank you."

"I couldn't have done it without you, Zorlo," Mia said, patting his furry arm.

Zorlo smiled, revealing a row of small, sharp teeth. "Mia," he began, "We, Xantorians, have a tradition. When someone does something extraordinary, we celebrate them with a Light Festival. We would like to **honor** you this way. Would you join us?"

Mia's eyes widened with surprise and excitement. "I'd be honored, Zorlo."

As the sun set, the Xantorians began their preparations. They gathered around a wide, open field filled with luminescent plants. In the middle of the field, a large platform made from **intertwined**, glowing vines was built. This was where Mia was asked to stand.

The festival started with music, a strange, beautiful melody produced by the giant tree-like creatures swaying in the breeze. Zorlo led Mia to the platform, and the crowd of strange but friendly creatures cheered.

Zorlo began to speak, "We gather here to honor Mia, our Earth friend, who saved our Heart, saved our planet. We are grateful."

With that, he signaled towards the sky. The Xantorians raised their six limbs, and a beautiful display of lights filled the sky. It was like nothing Mia had ever seen, even better than the fireworks on Earth.

Each creature **emitted** a bright light from their bodies, creating an amazing image of dancing lights.

Overwhelmed, Mia could only look on in awe, her face reflecting the dazzling lights of gratitude displayed before her. She felt a wonderful sense of friendship and was the happiest she had ever felt.

The celebration continued into the night, filled with laughter, stories, and a sense of shared joy. It was an experience Mia would carry with her forever.

As she looked at the sea of glowing faces, she promised herself she'd come back, not just because it was an adventure, but because she had found friends in this distant corner of the universe.

As the celebration finally came to an end, Zorlo walked Mia back to her spaceship.

"We will always remember this, Mia. And we will always remember you."

"And I will always remember you, Zorlo," Mia replied with a smile as she entered her spacecraft.

As her spaceship flew back to Earth, Mia couldn't stop smiling. This had been the best adventure of her life. Even in the dark, empty space, there were friends to be made and worlds to be saved. And she was ready for whatever came next.

New words

- **astronaut** *(noun)*: A person trained to travel in a spacecraft.
- **mission** *(noun)*: An important task or job that someone has to do.
- **swirling** *(verb)*: Moving in a twisting or spinning motion.
- **fascinating** *(adjective)*: Extremely interesting or charming.
- **crystal** *(noun)*: A clear, transparent mineral or glass resembling ice.
- **rumble** *(verb)*: To make a deep, long, rolling sound.
- **device** *(noun)*: An object or machine created for a particular purpose.
- **spongy** *(adjective)*: Soft and full of holes or spaces.
- **flora** *(noun)*: The plants of a particular region or period.

- **iridescent** *(adjective)*: Showing many bright colors that change with movement.
- **foliage** *(noun)*: The leaves of a plant or many plants.
- **undergrowth** *(noun)*: Small trees and plants growing beneath taller trees in a forest.
- **honor** *(noun)*: Respect or esteem that is given to someone or something; a privilege or reward.
- **intertwined** *(verb)*: To be twisted together or connected in a way that is difficult to separate.
- **emit** *(verb)*: To send out or discharge something such as light, heat, sound, or a smell.
- **overwhelmed** *(adjective)*: Having been given or faced with an excessive amount of something, such as emotions or tasks. Often used to describe feeling very emotional or stressed.

Test yourself

1. Who is Mia's best friend?
    a) Zorlo
    b) Ben
    c) The Heart of Xantoria
    d) The Power Pulsar

2. What is the 'Heart of Xantoria'?
    a) A device in Mia's spaceship
    b) A stone that gives energy to the planet
    c) A creature Mia met on the planet
    d) A plant on the planet

3. What device did Mia use to save the 'Heart of Xantoria'?
    a) A Power Pulsar
    b) A spaceship
    c) An energy stone

4. What is Zorlo?

    a) A robot

    b) An astronaut

    c) A planet

    d) A creature from Xantoria

5. What did Mia promise Zorlo at the end of the story?

    a) To bring more humans to Xantoria

    b) To come back to Xantoria

    c) To take Zorlo to Earth

    d) To take the Heart of Xantoria to Earth

Discussion

1. If you were to visit an alien planet like Xantoria, what would you be most excited to see or experience, and why?

2. What is the strangest place you've ever visited? How did it make you feel and why did you find it strange?

3. If you met an alien like Zorlo, what would be the first question you would ask them?

ANSWERS

1. b) Ben
2. b) A stone that gives energy to the planet
3. a) A Power Pulsar
4. d) A creature from Xantoria
5. b) To come back to Xantoria

Journey through Space

In the year 2084, life was busy on Mars. Mars was a lot like Earth now—humans had been living there for nearly 20 years. There were big cities full of people. These cities were under big clear **domes**, which helped people to breathe air just like on Earth. There were tall buildings and nice parks where people liked to spend time.

During the day, the sky on Mars was pink. It was illegal on Mars to have lights on at night, which meant the sky was always pitch black and the stars were incredibly beautiful and bright. The people living on Mars loved looking at these stars. They liked to dream about what was out there in space.

Among these people were Jake and Lily. Jake was an **engineer**. He loved to fix things. His friend Lily was a scientist. She loved to learn new things.

One day, while Jake was looking at his **radar**, he found a strange **signal**. It was coming from **Ganymede**, a moon far away. Elara, the leader of their city, asked Jake and Lily to find out more.

"We need to find out what is going on," said Elara. "And you two are the best people for the job."

So, they went on a space trip. They left Mars and went to Ganymede. The trip was scary but exciting.

Ganymede was unlike anything Jake and Lily had seen. This moon was colder than the coldest winter on Mars. Everywhere they looked, they saw ice. The ground was hard and slippery. Tall ice cliffs stood like frozen giants. Even the air was chilly and made them shiver.

Inside a massive ice cave, they found something they did not expect. It was a strange object, unlike anything they had seen. It was round and glowed softly. The object was covered in strange signs. It was clear that it was very old and not made by humans.

"It looks like it was made by aliens. It definitely wasn't made by humans," said Jake.

The object, when touched, showed a star map. The map pointed to a far-off place in space.

Now Jake and Lily had a big choice to make. They could go back to Mars or follow the star map.

"Going back is the safe choice, but following the map will be an adventure!" said an excited Lily.

After talking, they chose the adventure. They were ready for the **unknown**.

Their journey to the far-off place was hard. Space was not empty. There were rocks that moved fast. These rocks could hit their spaceship and there were times when the spaceship stopped working. Jake and Lily had to fix it again and again. It was scary, but they did not give up. They worked together. When one was tired, the other helped.

"You still think this was a good idea?!" asked Jake.

"Absolutely! What is life without adventure?" smiled Lily.

Finally, they reached a new planet. This planet was the home of strange **beings**. These beings were much taller than humans. They had shiny skin that looked like metal and they had six long arms.

The beings did not talk with sounds. Instead,

they shared thoughts. They could 'speak' directly into Jake and Lily's minds.

The beings were friendly and took Jake and Lily to their city. Their city was beautiful. It was full of bright colors and tall **towers** that touched the sky. The towers were made of a **material** that was shiny like glass but strong like metal.

Jake and Lily were given a place to stay. It was a round house with big windows. From the windows, they could see the whole city.

"This is the most beautiful thing I've ever seen!" said Lily.

"It really is incredible," Jake nodded in agreement.

In the days that followed, Jake and Lily spent time with the aliens. They were curious about these beings and their way of life. They noticed that the aliens lived in peace. They **respected** each other and their planet.

With time, Jake and Lily started to understand the aliens' thoughts. The aliens shared their history with Jake and Lily. They learned that the aliens had lived on their planet for a long time.

The aliens had built their city with the help of their advanced technology and they would always use the resources of their planet carefully.

The aliens also shared their knowledge about their technology. This technology was not like human technology. It did not harm the planet. Instead, it helped the planet. The technology used the power of the sun and the wind. It made the air clean and the water clear.

"I wish we treated our planet like this!" said Lily. "It just makes so much sense."

Not only did Jake and Lily feel like they had found new friends in a far-off place, but they had learned so much from them.

The more time they spent with the aliens, the more they understood them. They learned to respect the aliens and their way of life. They also learned how important it was to live in peace with nature.

As the time came for Jake and Lily to return to Mars, the alien friends provided them with helpful tools. These were not ordinary tools, but advanced alien devices.

There was a **solar converter**, a device that could take in sunlight and change it into energy. Then there was an **air purifier**, a device that made the air clean and safe to breathe. They also received a **water recycler**, a device that could make used water clean again.

The aliens taught Jake and Lily how to use these devices and gave them some extra tools to make their journey home safer.

The spaceship now had **shields** that could push away space rocks. It had a new **engine** that was more powerful. And the best part was that these improvements did not harm space.

Once they arrived on Mars, they were **greeted** with cheers and smiles. Their fellow Martians were so happy to see them again and excited to hear about everything they had learned.

Jake and Lily introduced the alien devices to their people. They **demonstrated** how the solar converter could generate energy from sunlight. They showed how the air purifier could make their domed cities' air fresher. They showed how the water recycler could make used water clean again.

Life on Mars began to change for the better. With the solar converter, they had a new way to power their homes and machines. With the air purifier, their air became cleaner, and breathing felt easier. The water recycler allowed them to have a **constant** supply of clean water.

Mars **evolved** into a healthier, happier place to live. The people had a new respect for each other and their planet. They were more caring and worked together to make Mars a better place.

Jake and Lily never stopped exploring, and over the years they worked hard to improve the planet they were proud to call home.

New words

- **dome** *(noun)*: Round structure that covers an area, used here to cover cities on Mars.
- **engineer** *(noun)*: A person who designs, builds, or maintains machines, bridges, etc.
- **radar** *(noun)*: A system that uses radio waves to find the position of objects that are far away.
- **signal** *(noun)*: A sound, image, message, etc. that is sent by radio, television, etc.
- **Ganymede** *(noun)*: A moon of Jupiter; it is the largest moon in the solar system.
- **unknown** *(noun)*: A thing that is not known, familiar, or understood.
- **beings** *(noun)*: Creatures or entities that exist.

- **tower** *(noun)*: Tall, narrow building or a part of a building that rises high above the ground.
- **material** *(noun)*: A solid substance from which things can be made.
- **respect** *(verb)*: To have a good opinion of someone because they behave well.
- **advanced** *(adjective)*: Modern and well developed.
- **solar converter** *(noun)*: A device that transforms sunlight into another form of energy.
- **air purifier** *(noun)*: A device that removes contaminants from the air.
- **water recycler** *(noun)*: A device that purifies used water, making it clean again.
- **shield** *(noun)*: Protective device or mechanism.
- **engine** *(noun)*: A machine that uses energy to provide power.
- **greet** *(verb)*: Welcome, usually with a particular action or words.

- **demonstrate** *(verb)*: Show how to do something.
- **constant** *(adjective)*: Happening all the time or regularly.
- **transition** *(noun)*: The process of changing from one condition or state to another.
- **evolve** *(verb)*: Developed gradually, especially from a simple to a more complicated form.

Test yourself

1. What was Jake's job on Mars?
- a) He was a teacher.
- b) He was an engineer.
- c) He was a scientist.
- d) He was a doctor.

2. Where did Jake and Lily find the alien object?
- a) On Earth.
- b) On Mars.
- c) On Ganymede.
- d) On the alien planet.

3. What was the alien object they found?
- a) A map to another planet.
- b) A weapon.
- c) A book.

4. How did the aliens communicate?
a) Through writing.
b) Through signs.
c) By sharing thoughts.
d) Through speaking.

5. What changed in life on Mars after Jake and Lily's return?
a) People stopped using technology.
b) Life became harder.
c) Life remained the same.
d) Life became better due to the new alien technology.

Discussion

1. Do you like adventures? What is the
   most adventurous thing you have ever
   done?

2. How important is it to you to protect our
   planet?

3. Would you like to live on Mars in the
   future? What do you think life would be
   like?

ANSWERS

1. b) He was an engineer.
2. c) On Ganymede.
3. a) A map to another planet.
4. c) By sharing thoughts.
5. d) Life became better due to the new alien technology.

The Interstellar Zoo

ara, a young university student with a fascination for the cosmos, was a bit of an **oddball** compared to her peers. When others spent sunny afternoons playing sports or socializing, Sara could be found lying on the grass, her eyes glued to the beautiful view of the sky above. She wasn't just daydreaming; she was observing, calculating, wondering.

Her obsession with the universe was not without its **detractors**, especially Professor Bernard, her **pragmatic** Physics instructor at the university. A firm believer in the here-and-now, he would often **reprimand** Sara for her '**head in the clouds**' approach.

"Miss Davies, your constant stargazing won't get you good grades," he'd say with a pointed look over his half-moon glasses.

Yet, Sara was **unperturbed**. The stars, planets, and the possibility of **extraterrestrial** life continued to fascinate her.

One sunny afternoon, a typical one with Sara lying on the grass, she noticed something **atypical**. A strange light appeared in the sky - a small, shiny object that looked sort of like an airplane. But this was no airplane or satellite. It was different. Its glow was unique, and the way it moved was uncharacteristic.

The most unusual thing, however, was that it seemed to be getting bigger, as if it were coming closer to Earth.

Ignoring Professor Bernard's words echoing in her head, Sara ran inside to fetch her telescope. Today wasn't just about gazing at the stars; it was about tracking this mysterious **celestial** object. As she focused her telescope on the bright object, her computer pinged with a new email.

It was from NASA, where she was registered for regular updates, but this one was different.

The email was marked "Top Secret: For Your Eyes Only."

The email read, "Dear Sara, we've noticed the same object you're observing. We believe it's an alien spaceship. We need your help to communicate with them. Please keep this secret."

With wide eyes and a rapidly beating heart, Sara began typing on her computer, sending messages to the spaceship. To her amazement, they responded. They declared themselves as peaceful explorers, curators of an "Interstellar Zoo," a spaceship filled with unique and wondrous creatures from across the universe.

"We need your help," the aliens requested. "Our spaceship is experiencing difficulties. We need to land on Earth and find a safe place for our animals. Can you assist us?"

Without wasting a moment, Sara sent them the coordinates of a large, empty field nearby. Within a matter of hours, the spaceship smoothly landed, the ground trembling beneath Sara's feet. The extraterrestrial beings expressed their gratitude and invited Sara on board to tour the Interstellar Zoo.

As Sara stepped aboard the spaceship, she found herself surrounded by a surreal spectacle, an extraordinary **menagerie** of creatures from the farthest corners of the universe.

To her left, a gigantic, purple elephant was gracefully floating in a gravity-free enclosure.

The creature, unlike any elephant Sara knew from Earth, was entirely weightless, its huge body twinkling with a million stars embedded within its thick, glowing skin. As it moved, its body rippled like a **mirage**, and its eyes radiated a gentle, welcoming warmth that was strangely calming.

On her right, a clear case housed a tiny dragon, but unlike the fire-breathing monsters of Earthly legends, this creature exhaled gusts of frosty air. Each breath it released turned into beautiful snowflakes. Its scales shone like polished diamonds, and its wings, though very small, seemed powerful enough to cause a hurricane. Sara found herself **entranced** by the mesmerizing beauty of this ice-breathing miniature dragon.

And then there was the beautiful bird, perched on a branch of what looked like a neon tree. It was no ordinary bird. Its feathers shimmered with a luminosity that could put the **Northern Lights** to shame. Each feather was like a tiny prism, breaking light into brilliant colors that danced and changed with the bird's every movement. As it spread its wings, a dazzling array of colors filled the spaceship, painting the entire Interstellar Zoo in colors of the cosmic rainbow.

Sara was speechless, her breath taken away by the astonishing array of alien creatures around her. It felt as though she had become part of a living, breathing piece of cosmic art.

"Oh no," one of the alien hosts exclaimed. "One of our animals is suffering. It requires a specific food source to survive, but we've **exhausted** our supply."

Sara's heart ached at the sight of the distressed creature. She asked about the creature's diet, and the alien explained it was a rare fruit native to a distant planet, but the **nutritional composition** was what mattered most.

In that moment, a glimmer of hope sparked

in Sara. She remembered Professor Bernard had been researching a **synthetic** food source designed to match the nutritional composition of a similar extraterrestrial fruit. It was meant to help astronauts during long-duration space missions. What if it could also help this creature?

Sara declared, "I have an idea. My Professor has been working on a food source that could match the nutritional needs of your animal. But we need the exact nutritional composition."

With the alien's help, Sara obtained the specific nutritional profile. She immediately called Professor Bernard and explained the situation. He was initially **skeptical**, finding the story of an interstellar zoo quite hard to believe. However, Sara's insistence and the complex nutritional data she forwarded persuaded him that it was worth a try.

Working late into the night, they managed to create a batch of the synthetic food source, designed to replicate the nutritional complexity of the rare alien fruit. Exhausted but **triumphant**, Sara and Professor Bernard, armed with their synthetic fruit substitute, arrived at the landed spaceship the following morning.

The spaceship hummed with a strange sort of approval as they entered, the solution to their problem in hand. The journey to the distant planet was no longer necessary.

As the alien creature calmed down, munching contently on the synthetic fruit, a sense of relief washed over the spaceship. Professor Bernard, standing beside Sara, looked at her with a **newfound** respect. He saw the passion, intelligence, and courage in this young woman that he had previously dismissed as simple daydreaming.

"Sara," he said, turning to her. "I owe you an apology. I've often said that you spent too much time with your head in the clouds, looking at stars. But today, I've seen firsthand where that passion can lead, the good it can do." He gestured at the now happy and healthy creature. "You've not only helped this creature but also opened my eyes. Your dreams of the cosmos, your curiosity... they're not a waste of time. They're valuable, essential even. Keep reaching for the stars."

With that, Sara's heart filled with joy. Not only had she helped save the interstellar zoo, but she had also proved that her dreams, her love for the cosmos, was worthwhile. With newfound determination, she looked up at the stars that night, knowing she had friends up there, and a bright future ahead of her.

New words

- **oddball** *(noun)*: A strange or eccentric person.
- **detractor** *(noun)*: A person who criticizes something or someone, often unfairly.
- **pragmatic** *(adjective)*: Dealing with problems in a practical and sensible way rather than by having fixed ideas or theories.
- **celestial** *(adjective)*: Of or relating to the sky or outer space.
- **extraterrestrial** *(adjective)*: Originating, existing, or occurring outside the earth or its atmosphere.
- **menagerie** *(noun)*: A collection of different animals kept especially to be shown to the public.
- **mirage** *(noun)*: Something that appears real or possible, but is not in fact so.

- **entranced** *(verb)*: Filled with delight or wonder.
- **nutritional composition** *(noun)*: The breakdown of the nutrients contained in a food or substance, including elements like proteins, fats, carbohydrates, vitamins, and minerals.
- **synthetic** *(adjective)*: Made by chemical synthesis, especially to imitate a natural product.
- **triumphant** *(adjective)*: Being victorious or successful.
- **newfound** *(adjective)*: Recently discovered or established.
- **unperturbed** *(adjective)*: Not worried or anxious; staying calm.
- **reprimand** *(verb)*: To tell someone officially that something they have done is very wrong.
- **exhausted** *(verb)*: To have used up or consumed completely; to have drained of energy or vitality, often referring to a

person feeling extremely tired or worn
out.

- **head in the clouds** *(phrase)*: To be not
  paying attention to what is happening
  around you because you are thinking
  about something else. Often used
  to describe someone who is often
  daydreaming or lost in their own
  thoughts.
- **atypical** *(adjective)*: Not typical; not
  usual or normal.
- **entranced** *(verb)*: Filled with wonder
  and delight, to the point where you can't
  focus on anything else.
- **Northern Lights** *(noun)* - Natural
  light displays in the Earth's sky,
  predominantly seen in the high-
  latitude regions (around the Arctic and
  Antarctic).
- **skeptical** *(adjective):* Having or showing
  doubt or disbelief; questioning the
  validity or authenticity of something.

Test yourself

1. What was Sara fascinated by?
    a) Sports
    b) Socializing
    c) The cosmos

2. What was the strange light that Sara saw in the sky?
    a) A new star
    b) A satellite
    c) An airplane
    d) An alien spaceship

3. Why did the alien spaceship need to land on Earth?
    a) To give Sara a tour.
    b) Their spaceship was experiencing difficulties and they needed a safe place for the animals.
    c) They wanted to contact humans.

4. Who helped Sara create the synthetic food for the scared creature?

       a) Her parents

       b) The aliens

       c) Her university professor

       d) Her friends

5. How did Professor Bernard's opinion of Sara change by the end of the story?

       a) He still thought she wasted too much time daydreaming.

       b) He thought she was very brave and intelligent.

       c) He thought she was still an oddball.

       d) He did not change his opinion about Sara.

Discussion

1. Have you ever been doubted by a teacher or another person, similar to how Professor Bernard doubted Sara? How did you prove them wrong?

2. If you were in Sara's position, would you have acted the same way when you saw the alien spaceship? Why or why not?

3. What is something you are passionate about, and how does it influence your actions and decisions in your life?

1. c) The cosmos.
2. d) An alien spaceship.
3. b) Their spaceship was experiencing difficulties and they needed a safe place for the animals.
4. c) Her university professor.
5. b) He thought she was very brave and intelligent.

The Shooting Star Pendant

Once upon a time, in a faraway place in space, there lived a brave and adventurous woman named Alex. Since she was young, Alex loved space and its secrets. As a child, she would lie under the sky full of stars, dreaming about other planets and exciting adventures she could have.

As she got older, Alex read old books and **futuristic** stories, learning about lost planets and old civilizations. Every night, her room glowed with pictures of stars on the walls.

When she was old enough to go on her own journey, Alex spent three years building her own spaceship, which she called Stardust. The ship was shiny and strong.

The most impressive thing about Stardust was its intelligent computer system called AURA. AURA was incredibly smart and became like a best friend to Alex.

Alex and AURA went on special space adventures together. Her mission was to

learn and discover and share what she found with her friends and family back home.

Together, they traveled to Saturn's rings, where she was amazed by the giant planet and its pretty moons. Alex flew through rocks in space and went into nebulae where stars were born.

As Alex's love for discovery grew, she often looked at stars dying and new ones being born, feeling amazed at how big and beautiful everything was.

One calm day, a bright light caught Alex's eye. "Look! A shooting star!" she said, excitedly. As they got closer, something strange caught her attention.

Among the rocks, there was a small, shining object like a special jewel—it was a beautiful sapphire blue color, but it certainly wasn't just a sapphire. Alex was so curious that she had to see it closer. As she got closer, she could see that inside of it looked like a miniature universe with thousands of twinkling stars. It was beautiful.

When she touched it, a strong cosmic energy went through her. "Whoa! What's happening?" Alex said, surprised and confused.

AURA said, "This is not normal, Alex. It has a special power, but we don't know what it is."

The necklace kept glowing, and Alex's mind was filled with strange ideas. As she watched the necklace, she realized it could control how things move in space. It could change the **gravitational force** of an object. When you live in space, this power was incredibly powerful. It was wonderful but also very dangerous.

Wanting to understand it better, Alex began to play with the necklace's powers. She made small objects in the ship float and dance around, laughing as they spun in the air.

She even used the power to create shapes and patterns with the stars outside the ship's window, turning them into twinkling pictures. It was like drawing with the universe itself!

Alex's heart was filled with joy as she discovered the fun side of this magical necklace. It wasn't all dangerous; it was also a tool for creativity and fun.

Suddenly, AURA lit up with bright flashing red lights, shocking Alex.

"Warning, an unknown **fleet** is coming our way," exclaimed AURA.

"Unknown fleet? What does that mean?!"
Alex asked, nervously.

AURA added, "They are not friendly! Get
ready, Alex."

Alex quickly turned on Stardust's shields, and
an **epic** space battle began. The other ships
shot powerful **surges** of energy at them, but
Alex fought back.

"Let's see what this necklace can do!" she
said, connecting it to the ship. Stardust
became faster and stronger. "We're winning
now!" Alex yelled, defeating the enemy ships
one by one, before none were left.

"That was easy—and so much fun!" giggled
Alex.

But just as she was about to relax, she saw
something **menacing** in the distance.

"We've found a big problem," AURA warned. "That is an ancient warship that has been in many battles. It has never lost a battle and it is very dangerous."

"Oh no! This is going to be hard," Alex said, scared.

Alex gripped the controls of the Stardust tightly, knowing that what lay ahead would be a battle unlike any she had ever faced. Her heart pounded with a mixture of fear and excitement as she prepared to confront this unexpected and formidable challenge.

The big ship attacked, and Stardust had to escape. "We can't fight this ship, it's too powerful!" Alex said. "We have to use the necklace again!"

She used the necklace to attack the huge ship. "Fire everything!" she said, and the huge ship broke apart in a spectacular explosion that created cosmic fireworks in the sky.

The battle was won, but Alex knew the necklace was too powerful. If it got into the wrong hands, it could be misused.

She decided to keep it safe and only used it if she had hostile situations to **conquer**.

Alex and AURA continued their journey through the stars, looking for new things to learn, while **casually** saving the universe along their way, of course.

New words

- **futuristic** *(adjective)*: Relating to, or involving very modern technology or design, often from an imagined future time.
- **sapphire** *(noun)*: A precious gemstone, typically blue.
- **gravitational force** *(noun)*: The force that pulls objects towards each other due to their mass. It's the force that holds planets, stars, and galaxies together and causes objects to fall to the ground on Earth.
- **fleet** *(noun)*: A group of ships, vehicles, or aircraft operating together under the same ownership or control.
- **epic** *(adjective)*: Heroic or grand in scale or character; relating to a long poem telling the story of a hero.
- **surge** *(noun)*: A sudden and strong increase or burst of something, such as wind, water, sound, or emotion.

- **menacing** *(adjective)*: Suggesting the presence of danger; threatening or frightening.
- **conquer** *(verb)*: To overcome and take control of a place or people by the use of force; to successfully deal with or gain control of something difficult.
- **casually** *(adverb)*: In a relaxed and unconcerned manner; without apparent effort or fuss.

Test yourself

1. What was the name of the spaceship Alex embarked on her journey?
    a) Sunbeam
    b) Stardust
    c) Starlight

2. What did the shooting star necklace have the power to control?
    a) Time
    b) Electricity
    c) Gravity

3. What did Alex do when faced with the huge warship?
    a) Flee
    b) Surrender
    c) Use the pendant to protect the Stardust

**4. What was the reason behind Alex's
intergalactic journeys?**
       a) To conquer new planets

       b) To gain power and control

       c) To learn

       d) To defeat hostile fleets

**5. What was Alex's reaction when she
discovered the shooting star necklace?**
       a) Fearful and hesitant

       b) Surprised and confused

       c) Indifferent and uninterested

       d) Angry and annoyed

Discussion

1. If you were in Alex's position and stumbled upon the magical necklace, how would you feel? What choices would you make, and how do you think it would affect your adventures in space?

2. Imagine having the power to control gravity. How would you use this power? What potential consequences or responsibilities would you consider?

3. Do you think humans will be living in space and driving spaceships in the next 200 years? Why or why not?

1. b) Stardust
2. c) Gravity
3. c) Use the pendant to protect the Stardust
4. c) To satisfy her insatiable thirst for knowledge
5. b) Surprised and confused

A Journey Beyond the Pages

Max was an **unassuming** man, who lived in a pretty average city. He was of average height, with a head of messy dark hair and a pair of hazel eyes that sparkled with **curiosity**. By day, Max had a boring job at the local post office, diligently tapping away at his keyboard, but his true self came alive when the sun went down.

Each evening, as the city lights turned on and the skies were painted with hues of orange and purple, Max's transformation began. With the closing of his apartment door, he stepped into his sanctuary – a cozy, book-lined **haven** that held the secret to his extraordinary passion. There, on the old wooden bookshelf

that covered an entire wall, lay a **trove** of treasures – his beloved science fiction books.

Every night, like clockwork, Max embarked on amazing journeys of the mind, escaping into the mesmerizing realms of alien planets, interstellar battles, and futuristic technologies.

His heart would race with excitement as he delved into the pages, traveling **light-years** away from the boring reality of his tiny apartment and into the limitless **expanse** of the cosmos.

Through the power of words, Max's imagination soared. He roamed with **intrepid** explorers across new territories, encountered inspiring alien civilizations, and witnessed the birth of magnificent celestial **phenomena**.

With every turn of the page, he became a witness to epic battles between the forces of good and evil, each tale a symphony of emotions that had him wanting more.

Within the enchanting confines of those sci-fi stories, Max found a true sense of belonging. In the soft glow of his bedside lamp, he formed unbreakable connections with characters he considered to be his true companions. Captain Nova's **unwavering** determination, Luna's insatiable curiosity, and even the quirky but endearing alien crew members, Pogo and Krell, all had a place in Max's heart.

His passion for sci-fi grew stronger every day. It was more than a hobby; it was his escape from the **monotony** of everyday life.

Yet, despite his love of these fictional universes, Max's reality remained unchanged. He **yearned** for an adventure of his own, a chance to experience the thrill of space exploration, to meet beings from distant galaxies, and to experience in real-life the cosmic wonders he read about.

Little did he know that his deepest desire was about to come true.

One day, while Max was engrossed in his

latest space epic, something extraordinary happened. As he turned the page of his book, a mysterious surge of energy **enveloped** the room, and before he knew it, the characters from the book appeared before his eyes. Shocked and bewildered, Max couldn't believe what was happening.

In front of him stood Captain Nova, a brave space explorer with a rugged charm, and Luna, a brilliant scientist with an insatiable curiosity. The alien crew members, Pogo and Krell, also appeared, each with unique abilities and personalities. Max's jaw dropped as he realized that his favorite sci-fi book had come to life!

Captain Nova, taking the lead, looked at Max and said, "Greetings, Earthling! We need your help to defeat the evil Drakon Empire and save the universe from impending doom!"

Max's heart raced with excitement. He had always dreamed of being part of a daring adventure like the ones he read about, and now it was happening for real! "Count me in!" he exclaimed, ready to face any challenge that lay ahead.

The newly formed team quickly set out on their mission, traveling through a **portal** that appeared in Max's living room. They found themselves in a dazzling spaceship, the Starfire, which could travel through galaxies in the blink of an eye. Max was in awe as he explored the futuristic vessel and met the quirky yet brilliant crew members.

As the Starfire soared through the cosmos, they encountered thrilling obstacles, daringly escaped meteor storms, and had thrilling space fights with the Drakon's menacing ships. Max couldn't believe how much he was enjoying his real-life sci-fi adventure!

However, in the midst of their **escapades**, an unexpected problem arose. The Starfire's core began to malfunction, threatening to tear the ship apart. Luna worked tirelessly, but the situation seemed dire.

"What do we do, Luna?" Max asked, trying to hide his concern.

Luna's eyes sparkled with determination. "We need a rare element to fix the core, Max. It can only be found on the forbidden planet of Cephoria, guarded by **treacherous** beings."

Captain Nova added, "It won't be easy, but we have no choice. We must go to Cephoria."

As the Starfire approached the eerie, dark planet, Max's heart pounded. He knew this was a dangerous mission, but he was ready to face it alongside his newfound friends.

The team landed on Cephoria, facing hostile creatures and navigating treacherous landscapes. Max's sci-fi knowledge came in handy, as he recalled strategies from the books he had read. He felt like a true hero, fighting side by side with Captain Nova, using futuristic gadgets, and solving complex puzzles.

Finally, they reached the heart of the forbidden planet, where the rare element was rumored to be. But to their surprise, they encountered a massive **guardian** creature that protected the precious resource. The beast was fearsome, with **colossal** wings and eyes that glowed with ancient power.

Pogo stepped forward, ready to negotiate with the guardian. Using her unique telepathic ability, she connected with the creature's mind, learning of its origins and intentions. To everyone's astonishment, the guardian turned out to be a guardian of wisdom and protector of knowledge.

Moved by Max's passion for sci-fi books and his **thirst** for knowledge, the guardian agreed to share the rare element. It recognized that Max's love for stories had kindled a deep appreciation for the universe's wonders and secrets. The team gathered the element, grateful for the unexpected ally they had found.

Back on the Starfire, the crew repaired the damaged core, and the ship's systems hummed to life. The adventure was far from over, but they had overcome a significant **hurdle.**

As the Starfire sailed through space, Max and his friends faced dangerous challenges from the evil Drakon Empire.

"Captain Nova, there's something strange ahead," Max warned, peering at the distant fiery Nebula of Svaria.

Captain Nova squinted, "Prepare for battle, everyone! The Drakons won't hold back."

The Drakon **armada**, led by General Xarok, launched a surprise attack on the Starfire, trying to capture its advanced technology.

"Shields up! We can do this together," Captain Nova commanded.

Luna used her knowledge, "I've found their weak points. Max, relay the information to everyone!"

Feeling brave, Max took charge, "You got it, Luna! Team, let's give them all we've got!"

In an exciting fight, the Starfire unleashed a

barrage of energy blasts that crippled the Drakon ships' shields.

Pogo's telepathic ability created confusion among the enemy, "They can't handle our combined strength!"

Krell sneaked into the Drakon flagship, "I'll disable their weapons from the inside!"

As the tide of battle turned, the Drakon fleet **retreated**, stunned by the Starfire's might and the unity of its crew.

But Captain Nova knew the fight was far from over, "Stay alert, everyone. The Drakons won't back down."

Next, they faced the Drakons' traps in the Enigma Nebula, where danger lurked in the beautiful luminescent crystals.

"Luna, any ideas on how to navigate this labyrinth?" Max asked.

"Max, follow my lead, and we'll make it through safely," Luna replied, guiding the ship expertly.

On the Drakon side, they discovered the enemy mining crystals for a deadly weapon.

"We have to stop that weapon," Captain Nova said. "Any suggestions, team?"

Max and Luna worked together, "We can redirect the weapon's energy back into the nebula."

Pogo and Krell provided a crucial distraction, "Leave it to us to create some chaos among their guards."

The weapon was sabotaged, causing the Drakon stronghold to **tremble**.

Back on the Starfire, they watched the nebula's brilliant colors dance and pulse, a testament to their victory.

As their journey progressed, Max and his friends discovered amazing galaxies and helped **oppressed** races.

"It's heartwarming to see the hope we bring," Luna said, looking at the grateful beings they had aided.

Through their adventures, they formed unbreakable bonds and became like a family. When the final confrontation with General Xarok came, Max stared into his eyes, "You may have power, but we have friendship and unity."

In a stunning final twist, General Xarok surrendered, understanding the beauty of life.

"Join us, General. There's a chance for **redemption**," Captain Nova offered.

As the dust settled and the stars shone brightly, the Drakon Empire was no more.

Max felt a twinge of sadness, saying goodbye to his newfound family, "We've been through so much together."

Captain Nova smiled, "And we've changed the universe for the better. We'll always be connected."

As they bid their farewells, Captain Nova handed Max a small, glowing crystal. "This is a token of our gratitude and a reminder of the adventure you brought to life. Never stop imagining, exploring, and seeking knowledge."

With tears in his eyes, Max embraced his newfound friends one last time before they returned to the pages of the book from whence they came. The portal closed, and Max was back in his living room, book in hand, but forever changed by the incredible journey he had lived.

From that day forward, Max's love for sci-fi remained as strong as ever, but he also learned that the most incredible adventures could be found not only in books but in the boundless possibilities of life itself.

And so, dear reader, whether you are young or old, never stop dreaming, imagining, and letting your love for stories come to life. The universe is full of wonders waiting to be discovered, and who knows, one day, your own adventure might just begin.

New words

- **unassuming** *(adjective)*: Not drawing attention to oneself; modest or humble.
- **curiosity** *(noun)*: A strong desire to know or learn something.
- **haven** *(noun)*: A safe and peaceful place; a refuge.
- **trove** *(noun)*: A collection of valuable or delightful items.
- **mesmerizing** *(adjective)*: Captivating or fascinating in a way that holds one's attention.
- **light-years** *(noun)*: A unit of astronomical distance equivalent to the distance light travels in one year, used to measure vast cosmic distances.
- **intrepid** *(adjective)*: Fearless and adventurous; brave.

- **phenomena** *(noun)*: Observable facts or events that are typically considered unusual or unexplained. They can be natural occurrences or something observed in various scientific disciplines. The singular form of the word is "phenomenon."
- **monotony** *(noun)*: Lack of variety and interest; tedious repetition and routine. It refers to something that is boring because it is always the same.
- **yearn** *(verb)*: To have an intense feeling of longing for something, typically something that is difficult or impossible to obtain. It refers to a strong desire or wish for something that you want very much but may not be able to have.
- **envelope** *(verb)*: To surround or cover something completely. It refers to being completely enclosed or encased, often in a gentle or protective way. For example, "The fog enveloped the town" means

that the town was completely covered in fog.

- **treacherous** *(adjective)*: Hazardous and dangerous; involving betrayal or deceit.
- **thirst** *(noun)*: An intense desire for something, including water.
- **hurdle** *(noun)*: A challenge or obstacle that must be overcome.
- **redemption** *(noun)*: The action of saving or being saved from sin, error, or evil.
- **portal** *(noun)*: In science fiction and fantasy, it refers to a magical or technological gateway that connects two distant locations, dimensions, or points in time. For example, "He stepped through the portal into another world" describes a person using a special gateway to travel to a different place or dimension.
- **expanse** *(noun)*: A wide and open area or surface; a vast extent of space.

- **tremble** *(verb)*: To shake involuntarily, typically as a result of fear or excitement.
- **unwavering** *(adjective)*: Firm and steady; not changing or faltering.
- **escapade** *(noun)*: Exciting, adventurous, or mischievous activity or adventure.
- **colossal** *(adjective)*: Extremely large or massive in size, extent, or degree.
- **guardian** *(noun)*: A person who protects, keeps watch over, or takes care of another person or something.
- **armada** *(noun)*: A large fleet of ships, especially warships, often organized for a specific purpose such as battle or exploration. The term is typically used to describe a powerful and imposing collection of naval vessels.
- **retreat** *(verb)*: Move back or withdraw, especially from something dangerous or unpleasant.
- **oppressed** *(verb)*: Subjected to harsh and unjust treatment or control.

Test yourself

1. What was Max's true passion?
    a) Painting
    b) Playing sports
    c) Reading science fiction books
    d) Cooking

2. What happened when Max turned the page of his book?
    a) The book disappeared.
    b) Characters from the book came to life.
    c) Max fell asleep.
    d) Max's apartment caught fire.

3. Where did Max and his friends encounter the first challenge from the Drakon Empire?
    a) The Enigma Nebula
    b) The Forbidden Planet of Cephoria
    c) The Fiery Nebula of Svaria

4. How did Max and his friends disable the Drakon's doomsday weapon?
    a) By destroying the weapon.
    b) By negotiating with the Drakon leader.
    c) By redirecting its energy back into the nebula.

5. What happened to General Xarok at the end of the story?
    a) He was defeated in battle .
    b) He joined Max and his friends on their journey.
    c) He escaped and vowed revenge.

Discussion

1. Share any personal experiences with books that have had a significant impact on you.

2. Max formed deep bonds with Captain Nova, Luna, Pogo, Krell, and the other crew members during their adventure. How do you think shared experiences can create strong connections between people? Have you ever had a similar bonding experience with others?

3. Do you have a favorite book, which you wish you could experience in real-life? Which one, and why?

ANSWERS

1. c) Reading science fiction books.
2. b) Characters from the book came to life.
3. c) The Fiery Nebula of Svaria.
4. c) By redirecting its energy back into the nebula.
5. b) He joined Max and his friends on their journey.

Great work! Why not check out our other books? Here are a few you might like:

Available now in all major online bookstores.

Join us!

Are you ready to take your English learning journey to the next level? Then join our private **Facebook community** of fellow learners! It's a friendly and supportive space where you can share, learn, and practice English.

Just scan the QR code and you'll be taken straight to our Facebook page. See you there!

facebook.com/groups/learnenglishhub

Thanks for reading this book. We hope you've had a great time with it and improved your English!

As authors, we're always eager to hear what you think, so we'd love it if you could take a moment to leave a review. Your honest feedback helps us improve our writing and also helps other readers decide if this book is right for them. Plus, we'd just really appreciate it!

Visit us at
www.bellanovabooks.com
for more great books to continue your learning journey.